Formatting Manuscripts

Plus Other Words of Advice

by

Tina Foster

To all writers who want to present a great looking and professional manuscript when submitting to acquiring editors at traditional publishing houses as well as to literary agents. May this book prove useful in your journey to publication.

Original version published in 2006

This is an updated and revised edition.

Author's Note

This book was written to help those writers who plan to submit to traditional publishers and their acquiring editors, as well as to literary agents. If you are planning to self-publish, then the formatting for a self-published book requires a whole new set of skills. But for those who wish to go the traditional route, then this is the book for you. It covers formatting as required by most of the traditional publishers, their editors, and most literary agents who deal with traditional publishers.

For those who don't know the difference, a ***traditional publisher*** is one who <u>pays you</u>, the author, for the privilege of publishing your work.

Self-publishers, or vanity presses as they are sometimes known, usually require <u>you to pay them</u> an up-front fee in order to publish your work.

The problem with this is that a writer can self-publish their own work, no matter how awful the writing. This is why self-published works sometimes have a bad reputation.

So, keep in mind that if you wish to submit to literary agents or acquiring editors at a publishing house, there is a standard which they expect writers to know before they submit their work for perusal. If you follow these guidelines you will have a nice looking manuscript that meets industry standards and is appreciated by editors and agents alike. Nothing thrills an agent more than to open a submission and see a nice looking, professional manuscript.

FORMATTING MANUSCRIPTS
Plus Other Words of Advice

Improper formatting is probably the ***first reason*** for rejection by most acquiring editors at a publishing house, as well as literary agents. They see the physical look of your manuscript as soon as they take it out of the package, ***before*** they even read one word of your story. If they see common beginning writer mistakes, your manuscript will go back into the package, ***unread.*** Proper formatting separates the professional writer from the amateur. Yes, there is an industry standard on how a manuscript should look, which editors and agents expect writers to know before they submit their manuscripts for perusal. Every writer should know these dos and don'ts of what editors and agents look for in a professional looking manuscript.

Believe it or not, there **is** an industry standard on how a manuscript should look. This is important for every writer to learn, because, ***before*** *an editor at a publishing house or a literary agent ever reads one word of your novel or story, the first thing they see is the physical layout of the manuscript, as soon as they take it out of the package.*

Here are the steps to **creating a properly formatted manuscript**. *Now I'm talking about a manuscript that you plan to send out to an Acquiring Editor at a publishing house or to a literary agent.* Not if you are formatting it for camera ready, or self-publishing, or e-publishing. That is a whole *different format* and they will tell you how they want your material formatted. But if you are submitting a printed copy of your manuscript for an editor or agent to consider, then you need to follow these steps.

Just as a note here, as a general rule, most editors and agents will **not** accept a full manuscript sent by email or sent on a disk, as they don't like to sit at their computer and read for hours at a time. Most prefer a **printed** copy that is properly formatted. However some agents have "gone green" and will now days take on a manuscript electronically. But you will have to email them for their **submission guidelines** to make sure this is okay with them.

Most traditional publishers still prefer a printed copy in proper format. If they like what you have written, they might invite you to send a copy on a disk for further consideration, and prior to offering you a contract. But until then, plan on submitting on paper most of the time.

Never send a copy of your manuscript by email or on a disk *unless specifically invited* to do so. Always plan on mailing a printed copy, and then only what they have specifically asked for, or as outlined in their submission guidelines. Usually they ask for the first three chapters and a short synopsis.

If they like what they read, they will invite you to send more. For more information on how to approach literary agents or Acquiring Editors, see my book on: ***"How to Write an Effective Query Letter," Plus Other Advice on Approaching Editors and Agents.***

If you get in the habit of setting up the format for your manuscript right from the start, before you even write one word of your story, it will save you going back and making hundreds of changes later on. It takes only a couple of minutes to set it up, and once you get in the habit, it will become automatic. Once your manuscript is properly formatted, the only changes you might have to make are the words themselves and sometimes the page numbers as you go through your various drafts.

Very seldom will someone create a perfect first draft. Plan on several drafts at the very least, and possibly dozens before your manuscript is honed and polished. But it will make your work a lot easier if you have your manuscript properly formatted right from the beginning.

Do NOT use Word Pad, or **NotePad or other similar programs** for writing a novel as these do not have the capabilities of a real word processing program. Use your *Microsoft Word* program or invest in *Corel Word Perfect*. These have more features than Word Pad or NotePad.

If you plan to publish electronically, you may have to convert *Word Perfect* to *Microsoft Word*. But if you are looking for a **traditional print publisher**, where they **pay you** for the rights to publish your work, then you need to follow the guidelines below on formatting your manuscript.

For those who decide to use a Print-on-Demand (POD) publisher, they will tell you how to set up your manuscript. They have conversion tools to help you. As do eBook publishers. For some reason, *Word Perfect* doesn't translate well to eBook format and can pick up a lot of corruption when converted, so if you plan to do an eBook version, you will have to use *Microsoft Word*.

If your computer doesn't come with a good word processing program, my best advice is to invest in a good one if you plan to do much writing and want your manuscript to look professional. *Word Perfect* is a good choice and many professional writers prefer it. The *Word Perfect Office X5* comes with *Microsoft Word* as well, also with a Thesaurus, Dictionary, Spell Check, and many other useful tools. And I don't get any commissions from *Word Perfect* for promoting it. I feel it is a superior program for writers to use. Very user friendly. Right now I use *Word Perfect Office X5 for Home and Students.* It does everything the older versions do, plus more. You can get one for about $59.00 at Sam's Club. Or if you know some writer friends, you can split it between you. You can download it onto three computers. Often places like Staples who retail it for more, will match Sam's Club prices.

But if you have *Microsoft Word* on your computer, or prefer to buy a copy of that, then *learn to use it*. It is very important for a writer to know their way around their word processing program. *Word* used to come standard on most PCs, but now I think you have to buy that as an extra as well.

Word is a good investment if you plan to publish an eBook. It converts well to the electronic format for Kindle or other eReaders. Whereas, *Word Perfect* does not convert as well into the eBook format directly. It takes some learning and patience to get rid of the corruption which happens in the conversion process. Thus I have both programs on my computer currently. There are other programs out there geared for writers as well. But these are the most popular. Whichever program or software you decide to use, take some time to learn your way around it.

Now, on to formatting your manuscript.

This type of format is for using **standard 8 ½ x 11 inch paper**. Your manuscript should be printed on regular white 8 ½ x 11 inch paper. Print on <u>**one side** of the page **only**</u>.

1. Start With the Margins.

The side margins should be 1.25 inches on both right and left sides. One inch at the very least, but **never** less than one inch. Preferably 1.25. Some editors like 1.5 inches. Editors like lots of white space in order to make editing notes and comments on your manuscript pages.

Leave the **bottom margin at 1 inch**. The top margin can be moved up a bit to make room for the **header**. One inch is okay, but you can move it to somewhere between 1 inch and ½ inch. **I like to set mine at about .75, or .65.** Whatever you choose, **make a note of it** so you will have all your following chapter files on the same setting. In other words, *you want all your pages to look the same*. Not some margins higher or some lower, but all exactly the same.

Make a note of the setting you choose for your margins so you will remember, and so that all your pages will look uniform. If you click onto your **Page Layout** tab you will find many options. From there you can set up your margins.

2. Next, Set Up the <u>Header</u>.

This is the writing you see at the top of the page in most books that tells the author's name, the title, and the page numbers. That's what you are going to set up at this time.

There is a margin on your header called the "Header Gutter." This refers to the amount of space between the header and the main text below it on the page. You want to have this about the *same as a **blank double-spaced line or a bit more***. I set mine at .365 or .414, depending on which one shows up on the screen. This is for ***Word Perfect***.

For ***Microsoft Word***, it is called the "Header Margin," and is usually set for 0.5. They are roughly about the same. Again whichever one you choose, make a note of it so all your chapters will look the same when printed out.

If you go to the **Insert** tab and click, you will see a box that features Headers and Footers, as well as Page Numbers. You can click on the **Page Number** box and it will bring up some options. I won't go into a lot of detail here, as there are several different ways to set up your **Header**, and the programs may vary. But you want to choose to have the page numbers appear on the **upper right side of the header**.

Again, it is important to know your way around your word processing program. If you're not sure, **go to your help feature**. With a bit of practice it will take less than a minute to do all this and save you a lot of time later on.

Next: **pick the font** to use in your header. *This is very important.* The font should match the one you use for your main text on the page (Courier New, or Times New Roman are the most common). We'll discuss the proper font later on.

Next: On the **left side of your header type in the title** of your story in all capital letters (CAPS). If it has a long title, just use a few key words. Follow the title with a **slash (/** like this), then **type in your last name**, the first letter capitalized only, the rest in lower case letters.

Type in the starting **page number in the upper right corner** of the header. This way all your information is at the **TOP** of the page where it can be seen at a glance.

Page 1 starts where your story starts. Your title page does not count as page 1, nor does your acknowledgment page. More on this later. If you have a Prologue, or Foreword, or Author's Note that comes in front of the first chapter, then start page 1 with whatever comes first. Do NOT count Tables of Content, as part of your page count, the Dedication page, or similar things like that. These go in later if your project is accepted for publication. At this point they just want to know if you can **write** and present a good story.

Some word processors allow you to include the word "Page" along with your page numbers, *Word Perfect* will do this.

For *Microsoft Word*, if you put the cursor in front of the page number, then you can type in the **Title/your last name, then space over to the left side of the header**. You can also type in the word **Page in front of the number**. Leave enough space to allow for your starting page number. Also, **allow for double digits or triple digits**, depending on the length of your project, so the type doesn't overlap. Make sure you match your page numbering in the correct font, also.

You can also hit the enter key a couple of times and this will move the margin down so that your Header doesn't sit right on top of your main text. For *Word*, it takes a bit of practice to learn to set up the Header, but as you get acquainted with it, things will get easier.

Don't use Roman Numerals to indicate page numbers. These can become awkward and confusing as the numbers get higher, and most readers aren't familiar with them after a certain point. Just use regular digits, as in Page 1, Page 2, Page 3 Page 4, and so on. Once you set your initial setting, your pages should automatically print each page in sequential order. Along with the title and your last name in the header.

Don't use "footers" for a manuscript. Editors and Agents prefer all the **information at the top of the page** where it can be seen at a glance. Don't make them search all over for the page numbers.

You can usually set the "**value**" of the number to start with whatever number you wish. So, if you are starting a new section or set of chapters, you can start with whatever page number you want. Just so the finished manuscript prints out in consecutive page numbers.

When this guide is published in electronic format it may become a bit confusing because eReaders can adjust their text sizes and the page is shrunk to only a few inches. So, the samples I have may not mean much by looking at them. In order to benefit from the examples, this book was meant to be read in a print version. Also, there is going to be several changes in font to show the differences. In an eBook, there is no distinction in fonts, so it will lose some of the effectiveness in that respect.

When properly set up, your header should look similar to this:

FLIRTING WITH DANGER/Foster   Page 23

Make sure there is at least a double-spaced line or
slightly more, between the header and the main text
on the page. You don't want your header sitting
right on top of the main text. Once you set up your
initial header, it should print the same on each
page, along with consecutive page numbers. Again, if
you're not sure how to do this, go to your **help**
feature.

Don't load up your header with copyright symbols,
dates, and other information that doesn't need to be
there. In this example, I've shown how the type
looks in the **Courier New** font, in **13 point** type, with
double-spacing.

Again, if you are reading this on a Kindle, the
font differences won't show up.

3. Now Click Back on Your Main Page And Select Your <u>Font</u>.

The most preferred fonts are **Courier New or Times New Roman**. The third is Ariel, (or Arial), but this is a lesser used font, and many editors **don't like it** because it doesn't have serifs. I would stick with one of the first two fonts.

The reason is, publishers consider a font which has serifs on the letters, as **easier for the eye to read**. A "serif" is the little stroke at the bottom, top, or sides of certain letters. For most readers, serifs on the letters, helps to draw the eye across the page easier than a font without serifs. Especially if reading for long periods of time. That's why you will seldom see a novel printed in the Ariel font. Thus manuscripts should be printed in a font with serifs on the letters.

They are most noticeable on certain letters such as, M m, N n, S s, T, H h, W w, K k, A, R r, Y y, I i, and others. If we make the letters larger, you will see the serifs. M, N, S, T, H, W, K, A, R, Y, I. Note the small stroke at the tops and/or bottoms of these letters. Those are **serifs**.

Compare these to the letters in the Arial font (this is a sample of Arial) that have **NO** serifs. A B C D E F G H I and so on. You can see the difference in this example. (Unless you are viewing this on a Kindle) This font is more popular for use on business cards or brochures. It is a crisp clean font, and has it purposes. But to read a **full novel or manuscript** in this font can be very tiring on the eyes. It doesn't allow for the eye to flow across the page as easily, and especially when doing a lot of reading. Thus, I would **never** use this font for a manuscript submission. And it could get you a rejection.

The reason Courier New is an accepted font is because it looks like the old style typewriter font, and has been used for years to estimate word counts at publishing houses. It is a "**non-proportional**" font (see below for more information on non-proportional). This was how manuscripts were typed out for years, and many publishers still like it as a preferred font.

This is a sample of how the **Courier New font** looks and prints out for me. **All font settings should be in at least 12 point type.** Anything smaller and the editor will toss your manuscript out. They don't like anything that is hard to read. Several of my writer friends have a problem with their Courier font printing out light, somewhat like a draft mode, so they use **13 point** type to make it stand out a bit more. Some programs don't have a 13 point setting, so you would be better off using Times

New Roman for your font, as it prints out fairly sharp and

is easy on the eyes to read.

A "non-proportional" font means that the letter "I"

takes up just as much space as the letter "W." The

Courier font is a "non-proportional" font, much like

the old typewriter fonts that were used before

writers had computers.

Most publishers now days prefer submissions in the ***Times New Roman*** font. This is a sample of Times New Roman and usually comes standard on most computers these days. If your novel is very long, using this font will tighten your page count. This is because the Times New Roman font is a **"proportional"** font and squeezes the letters together to fit the space.

So you actually wind up with more words per page than the standard of 250 words per page that editors go by when planning the amount of space needed for a novel or story. When using Times New Roman, your manuscript may run closer to 300 words per page.

By using the proper font and proper margins, you should get an average of 250 words in Courier New, to 300 words per page with Times New Roman, which is considered the industry standard. Make sure your font setting is **always in 12 point or 13 point**. You can go into the "custom" setting or "other" setting and get the 13 point type, but standard 12 point is very acceptable.

If your font prints out smaller than standard 12 point type for some reason, then set it for a larger one. Editors read *all day long* and anything that is smaller than 12 point type is very tiring on the eyes. A 13 Point type is often appreciated.

Never use novelty fonts, or colored paper, as this just irritates the editor or agent and marks you as an amateur. And will most likely get you a rejection.

4. Always Make Sure Your Main Text is Set for <u>Double-Spacing</u>.

If your font prints out tighter for some reason, you'll need to go into the "custom setting" or "other" setting and set it for a bit higher. But most programs have a double-space setting, or 2.0. ***Never, never, <u>never</u>** submit a manuscript that is "single-spaced" **to an editor or agent.** *They seldom will even bother to read it,* and will normally reject it outright. This tells them you are a beginner and have not done your research into proper manuscript formatting.

This is how **Times New Roman** looks **double-spaced and in 12 point type**. Editors will recognize if you use 1.5 spacing instead of 2.0, as it looks much tighter than this. They see typefaces all day long. They know fonts, they know line spacing and they know which size the text is printed in. Don't try to get more words on a page by cheating. They will know and recognize this, and it comes across as unprofessional.

Let's review here a bit.

Again, make sure you have nice <u>wide margins</u>, 1.25 is preferred over 1 inch on the sides. Make sure your <u>Header</u> is properly set up with the <u>Title/your last name in the left upper corner</u>, and consecutive <u>page numbers in the right upper corner</u>. Select a <u>proper font</u>, and set your line spacing for <u>double-spaced</u>, or 2.0.

Editors and agents like all the basic information at the <u>top</u> of the page— not at the bottom, so everything is right there at a glance. So they don't have to search all over the page for information and page numbers. Pages get dropped or shuffled.

It is amazing how many submissions agents get where the author has neglected to include a header with the last name or page numbers. Once taken out of the envelope, the agent won't know which author to send it back to, or to answer the query, if they don't know whose story it is. An agent may take several submissions at a time to a comfy chair with good lighting to read through. Without a last name on the pages, how are they to know which envelope it came out of, and who to address their response letter to?

Also, without page numbers, sections of the chapters may get out of order and the agent won't be able to tell how it should read. Accidents do happen, and pages get dropped. Without consecutive page numbers they will not bother to re-arrange the pages. This also tells them that this writer hasn't learned proper industry protocol, and will most likely get a rejection outright.

For these reasons, as stated above, is why agents and editors require a header with basic information, and consecutive page numbers on each manuscript page. I'll go into formatting a "Title Page" a bit later. But double check to make sure your manuscript is set up properly thus far.

Now that you have your basic set up with the margins and header in place, and a correct font, you are now ready to start your first chapter, or possibly the Prologue, Foreword, Author's Note, Preface, or anything that comes before **Chapter One.** You still set these up **exactly like you would start a chapter**.

5. Double Space Down One Third of the Page to Start Your Chapter.

Never start a chapter at the top of a page. Always <u>start partway down the page</u>. This goes for any consecutive chapters as well. Since 5 is an easy number to remember, **you can space down 5 lines (double-spaced)**. On the fifth line, **center** your cursor and type in your chapter heading<u>.</u> Such as Chapter One, or Prologue.

However, 8 blank lines works well also. Some like to use 10 lines. Whichever number of blank double-spaced lines you choose, **make a note of it so that you'll remember**, so that **ALL** your chapter headings will look **exactly the same** when printed out, not some higher or some lower. The idea is that you want your manuscript to look *uniform*.

It's best to <u>spell out chapter numbers</u>, rather than just use the digits. This is not a hard and fast rule, but just <u>looks more professional</u>. **Avoid Roman Numerals**, as these can get confusing the higher up they go.

Put your chapter heading in all caps, or you can use bold, or both. Or some writers like to **make the type** larger. Whichever you use, make sure all your chapter headings <u>look the same</u>.

Now **space down two more blank double-spaced lines**, return to the left side, TAB in to ***indent the first line of your starting paragraph*** and start typing your story. If you have a chapter sub-heading, or sub-title, it should be centered underneath in regular letters, the first of each in caps.

Do not put blank lines between the paragraphs.

This is a business letter format or more commonly used for How-To books such as this one, and is not suitable for a manuscript, or novel. Though I've used blank lines between my paragraphs in this instructional book, you would NOT do this for a novel manuscript that you present to an acquiring editor, or a literary agent.

Just INDENT the first line 4 to 7 spaces in each new paragraph and start typing. If you set your **tab** key or set up your paragraphs to automatically indent, it should do this each time you hit the **enter** key.

With *Microsoft Word* you can set it to **first line indent** to a certain amount of spaces, so that all you have to do is hit the Enter key and it automatically indents the start of the next line.

You can find this feature if you go to the **Paragraph box** on the **Home** tab and look for the tiny, hard to see box with an arrow in the bottom right corner of the Paragraph box. Click on that and look for **Indentation**, then **Special**, with a small box next to that. Click on **First Line**, then in the small box to the side set the amount, usually **0.3 works well**. This will give you a good indent.

If you are reading all this on an eReader, the font samples are not going to mean much. This book was set up to show how it looks on a printed page of 8 ½ x 11 inch size, which is what you should print your manuscript on.

Then you follow with your **type set for double-spacing** or **0.20**.

Therefore, if reading this in a print version, your chapter heading should look similar to the one below:

CHAPTER TWENTY-THREE

What Should I Do Next?

Notice how I spelled out the chapter number, rather than just used digits. Keep in mind that there should be a hyphen between numbers such as twenty-three. And note that <u>the sub-heading is one double-spaced blank line below the main chapter heading</u>.

Whichever you chose, be consistent throughout the entire manuscript. Make sure your chapter headings all look the same or uniform. Don't have some in caps, and some in non-caps, or some in bold, and some not. You want them to look uniform.

Once you have your chapter heading, you <u>hit the enter key **twice**</u> to space down **two blank lines**, (like I've shown here if you're reading a print version), return your cursor to the left side, hit the TAB key to **indent** four to seven spaces (the Tab key should automatically do this for you, if not, then set it so it does), then start writing. Do **not** just tab in two spaces, since this is a format for a **published** book. Editors like your paragraphs **well defined**. So they can see how well you mark certain sections for emphasis. Many times a short paragraph acts to emphasize certain passages.

Never just end a paragraph and start a new one without indenting. This type of format leaves the reader confused as to where one paragraph ends and the new one starts. Also, this style tends to resemble one **long block of type** which is un-inviting to the reader. In this case, the reader being that acquiring editor or literary agent you are trying to make a good first impression on.

Make sure you are in the proper font. And your line spacing is set for double-spaced (2.0).

The reason editors like a good indentation for starting new paragraphs is that it makes them more noticeable, than just using 1 space or 2 spaces. Four is a good amount and your indented first line should be no less than 4 spaces. Some writers will send in a submission with no indentations at all, to signal where the paragraph breaks are. This happens often in an emailed submission. I'll talk later on about emailed submissions.

Remember, the reader's eye needs a break. By having a nice 4 or 5 space indentation for each new paragraph, it creates a natural break for the eye.

Again, **DO NOT** put blank lines between the paragraphs. Just **indent** the first line of each new paragraph, as shown here.

Remember, you are **not** presenting the pages as camera ready as you would for self-publishing or for e-Publishing. You are presenting a **manuscript** for an editor or agent's perusal. If sold to a publisher, they will re-format your project to fit the

printer's specifications for the type of book you are presenting.

The purpose of double-spacing is so that the editor or agent can make comments or

edit marks between the lines or in the nice wide margins. Most likely, if accepted and

a contract offered, they will still want you to make some revisions, and edits to suit

them. It may go through several different editors during this process.

Once published, your novel will be in standard single-spacing and with the regular

2 space indentation as you usually see in published books. Remember, you are

presenting a **Manuscript** for their perusal, **not** the finished product.

Now onto the next section of formatting that you should know.

6. Start Each <u>New Chapter</u> on a <u>Fresh Page</u>.

Do not tack a new chapter onto the end of your last chapter.

<u>Start each new chapter one third down the page</u>. Just like I've explained above.

When you finish your first chapter, go up to **Insert**, then to **Page Break** and click. It will start you on the next new page. **Double-space down 1/3** of the page (5, 8, or 10 double-spaced lines), **cente**r your chapter heading, just like you did for the first chapter.

I know this is repetitive, but I run across this often, so it needs to be restated. Each new chapter should start on a fresh page, about 1/3 down the page, never at the top of the page. **And never stick a new chapter onto the end of the last chapter**. This is very tacky and does not look professional.

Be sure to leave a double-spaced blank line between the chapter **heading** and the start of your main text, like was shown in the sample above.

7. Other Rules to Keep in Mind.

Never "Justify" or align the right side margin.

In most of the text in this instructional book, I have left the **right side margins ragged** to show how a manuscript should look. However, **in this paragraph and the one below, I have used "justification" to show the difference in how the type looks**. It looks nice in a published book, but should *not* be used in a manuscript. **Justification** spreads the type out and also looks unprofessional in a manuscript. You **only** do this for camera ready pages that are going to the printers, **not** for presenting a **manuscript to an editor or agent. Always keep the right side margin ragged**. Remember, your manuscript **is not** supposed to look like it is ready for the presses, it is supposed to look like a *manuscript*.

"Justification" is when the type is spread out so that both the right margins as well as the left margins are all even. It looks nice in a published book, as it should. But for a MANUSCRIPT the type **should flush left only** with the right side margins looking **ragged**.

Indent the first line of each new paragraph. I know I just talked about this in the section above, but it bears repeating. The first line of each new paragraph should be indented the standard of 4 to 7 spaces. If your TAB key setting does not do this automatically, then set it so it does. Then all you have to do is tap your Tab Key to indent when starting a new paragraph. Or if using *Word* you can set it for **first line indentation** and all you have to do is hit the Enter key. And it will indent.

*Even the first line of a new chapter or scene change should be **indented***. I've seen writers leave this first line flush with the left margin because they've seen it done this way in a *published* book. Again, **this is a <u>manuscript</u>.** When it goes to the typesetter, they will design how it is supposed to look when published. **Your job is to present a polished and professional looking <u>manuscript</u>.**

Don't put blank lines between your paragraphs. Though I've put blank lines between the paragraphs in this instructional book, do NOT do this in a novel or genre fiction manuscript. Putting spaces between the paragraphs is a business letter format and not appropriate for a **manuscript**. You might do this for a "How-To" book, but not for a novel.

I can't tell you how many manuscripts I get where the writer makes the mistake of putting a blank line between paragraphs. This will get them an **automatic rejection** as I know they haven't taken the time to learn industry protocol and **proper formatting**. Also, using blank lines can become awkward and confusing, especially when using short snappy lines of dialogue. It starts to become ridiculous.

Though I have spaces between the paragraphs here, I also have 1.5, and single-spacing which you should **not** use on a manuscript. I'll repeat: **Blank lines between paragraphs can get really confusing, especially where there are short, lines of dialogue**. Again, *just start a new paragraph on the next line and **indent.***

Don't Have Long Running Paragraphs

Never go more than half a page without a paragraph break.

Break them up. Again, editors like lots of white space. Also, long blocks of type can look daunting to the reader. **Remember, the reader's eye needs a break too**. You want your page to look inviting. Keep in mind that the literary agent or Acquiring Editor at a publishing house is often the first audience toward getting your book published. They read all day long, so you want to keep your paragraphs looking nice and short. If you see long paragraphs running on for more than half a page, find a place to break them up and start a new paragraph.

<u>Use underlining to signify text that is to be set in Italics</u>.

Don't use your Italics setting. This is because if you should be asked to submit on a disk, many **disk readers won't recognize or read Italics, but they <u>will</u> recognize or read underlining**.

This also **signals to the typesetter** that this particular sentence, word, or passage should be typeset in *Italics*.

If you just use your Italics setting, it may not be noticed by the typesetter, as some Italics don't look too much different from the regular text, especially when in the Courier font. The underlining makes it stand out to the typesetter. You use underlining for foreign words or phrases, or to emphasize a particular word or passage, or sometimes to signify a direct thought inside a character's head when you *don't use* a tag such as: he thought. **But go easy on these**. Don't overdo the underlining. Keep it minimal.

Many publishers have **updated equipment that <u>will</u> recognize Italics**, but you may not know for sure which ones do, or if the one you have submitted to has this equipment. So it is best to <u>do it the old fashioned way</u>. This is pretty much the industry standard and lets most editors and agents know that you are aware of this.

However, if they specify in their submission guidelines that you can use your Italics setting instead of underlining, then go ahead and do this.

There are some publishers who like writers to use ***<u>both</u>*** the Italics setting and underlining. That way the typesetter can go through and just eliminate the underlining when ready to go to press.

I may not reject a manuscript because they didn't use underlining, but I will point it out to them as something they may have to do, which is go through their entire manuscript and change all the Italics into underlining before it can be submitted to an Acquiring Editor at a publishing house.

Remember, again, your manuscript is not supposed to look like the finished product. It is supposed to look like a ***manuscript.***

To signify a shift in time, a change in scene, or a change in the point of view character, you will need to signify or *show* a scene break.

Use three Asterisks (* * *) ten spaces apart, centered, or a single pound sign (#) centered. Or three pound signs centered: Something like this:

*   *   *

Or:

\#

Or

\#\#\#

If you just use a blank line to signify a scene break, it can be misconstrued as a typing error. Also, *if the break happens to come at the <u>top or at the bottom of a page</u>*, the editor may not know there is *supposed* to be a break there. It is best to signify with the Asterisks or Pound sign so they will know for certain that the break is intentional. Again, this also alerts the typesetter that there is to be a scene break at this particular place.

Once a manuscript has been accepted by the publisher, they will reformat your entire novel to fit their style and the printer's specifications. So, you should not try to have your manuscript resemble a published book.

Use standard double quotation marks when a character is speaking dialogue, but *NOT for direct thoughts*.

This can confuse the reader. Is he saying this out loud? Or is he thinking it?

Once you have established a character's **Point of View (POV)** then you won't need to use clumsy tags such as, **he thought, she thought**. Once the reader is **inside** a particular character's head, you don't need to say, *he thought to himself*. How else does one think, but to himself? So, avoid too many "thought" tags. Save the quotation marks for dialogue.

Also, pay attention to the rules regarding quotes within quotes. **Use single quote marks around a quote that is within a quote**.

Example: "Did Jane really say, 'get out of here' when you went to her house?" Jack asked.

<u>Use basic punctuation</u>.

Use two spaces after a period and the start of the next sentence. I know you see only one space after a period in published books, but they do this to conserve space. Again, you are presenting a *manuscript*. However, it is becoming more acceptable to use just one space. Whichever you use, *be consistent*. Don't have some sentences with one space after the period and others with two spaces or even three spaces. *Make sure they are **all** the same*.

I'll get manuscripts with anything from 1 to 4 spaces. These writers don't seem to know that it looks more professional when all your sentences *conform to a standard.* Though it may be a drudge to do so, you may have to go through your **entire** manuscript and look for places where you have just one space, rather than two, and put in the spaces after a period. It is important to train yourself when you are typing, to automatically **hit the space bar twice after a period**.

But again, one space is becoming more acceptable to many publishers. The point is to be consistent in your spacing after a period at the end of a sentence. Throughout your entire manuscript. This makes it look more pleasing to the eye and looks professional.

If you use *Microsoft Word*, there is a paragraph symbol up in the top of the Paragraph box. It looks like a backward P with two thin lines for the stem. If you click on that it will help you to see how many spaces you have between sentences, and even if you've put an extra space between words. This is your friend. Use this to help spot these problems and help make your manuscript look uniform.

Learn when to properly use a comma and other punctuation marks.

One of the best books on grammar and punctuation is ***"Elements of Style"*** by Strunk and White. This little book has all your basic grammar and punctuation rules in it. Every serious writer should have a copy close at hand. It's small and easy to look things up.

Start each new sentence with a Capital letter.

This may sound elementary, but I've received submissions where the writer neglected to do this. Often beginning writers don't think they need to go back and re-read what they've written, or correct mistakes. They think it is the editor's job to fix all their mistakes. The editor has a lot more work to do these days than fix your mistakes. So do agents. So remember, your manuscript needs to look error-free, and polished.

Most programs these days will automatically put a cap on the start of a new sentence, as long as you ended your last one with a period.

Proper names are always capitalized.

When using nouns like, father, mother, son, sister, etc., it can depend on how it's used. If you are using father as a proper name, then it should be capitalized. But when using the generic version, you use the lower case.

As in: "Can I go now, Mom?" This addresses the mom as a proper name, so it should start with a capital letter.

But if you said: "Eric's mom said to tell you 'hi,'" Jim said. This is a generic version and does not need to be capitalized. Notice the 'hi' is a quote within a quote.

Brand names should be capitalized also.

With brand names, you would capitalize things like Kleenex, Band Aid, Nike, Levis, etc. But when using the generic terms, you would use: tissues, bandages, tennis shoes, blue jeans, etc., which don't need to be capitalized. By the way, Fridge is short for Frigidaire, which is a brand name. The generic version would be refrigerator.

All punctuation goes <u>inside</u> the quote marks when a character is speaking.

Use a comma when following a quote with, he said, Jane said, or other dialogue tags.

Example: "I thought you were coming with me," John said.

Use a period when following a quote with an *action tag*.

Example: "Don't tell me what to do." John glared at her.

One common mistake is the use of a comma after dialogue when the character is laughing. Laughter is an **action**, and therefore should not be treated as a dialogue tag. It should be treated as an action and look like this:

"That was really funny." Mary laughed.

Or you can do something like this: "That was really funny," Mary said, then laughed.

<u>Dots and Dashes</u>:

<u>Dots</u> (ellipses) are used to signify a *fading out or trailing off* of speech or thought.

Use three in a row, with spaces between if it's inside a sentence . . . like this, or four if it is at the <u>end</u> of a sentence. . . .

I've seen beginning writers use a whole bunch............ like this. This is wrong.
Stick with the correct amount, only 3 as in . . .   Or I've often seen three used at the end
of a sentence as well. . .

Use a full <u>em dash</u>— if your computer has the capability, or two regular dashes
together if not. You use the dash to signify an ***abrupt interruption*** of speech or
thought. Or sometimes in a parenthetical phrase. Go easy on these. Don't overdo the
dashes.

If you just use a **single dash**, like this-it can look too much like a **hyphenated**
word.

Some computers, even with the two dashes together, will still look like only one–
as shown here, rather than a full em dash. If this is your problem, try using *three*
together— like this. It will usually make it long enough to look like the full em dash.

Also, *put a space **after** your dash* and before the next word to set them apart.
Don't connect them together with the dash. In the samples shown above, I have put a
space after each dash, except the single one, to show how it can be misconstrued as a
hyphenated word, rather than a full dash.

Therefore, your dash should look like this— with a space after it.

Some editors will connect the dashes with the words—like this. If that is their
style, and what they prefer to use, then this is okay as well. Each publisher has their
own way of doing things.

But your job is to make your manuscript looks as pleasing as possible by sticking
with the rules. Don't make up your own rules. You probably won't be rejected
because you used a dash the wrong way. But it helps to be conscious of the publisher's
style of doing things. Also, whichever way you choose, **be consistent throughout the
whole manuscript.**

If you really need help, refer to *"Elements of Style"* by Strunk and White. Or, you can refer to the big fat $40 book, **The Chicago Manual of Style** which is the book most publishers refer to. But for basic writing techniques, *"Elements of Style"* will work just fine.

Never use more than one exclamation point!!!

I used the three above for sarcasm and to make a point.

Do not overdo exclamation points! I've used several in this section just **to show how they can start to jump out at the reader when overdone**!

Using more than one smacks of amateur and does nothing more to get your point across!!!!

Also, save these for when a character is actually **shouting or screaming**, or for special emphasis! Beginners tend to overdo these, wanting to emphasize almost every sentence!

Understatement has more impact than using lots of exclamation points, and these should be saved for special emphasis.

I often see **exclamations used improperly**, such as: "I love you!" she whispered. In this case the character is whispering and the exclamation point should not be used.

Show with body language what your character is feeling, or doing. If I see several exclamations on a page, it smacks of beginner and I'll usually put down their manuscript.

Some writers avoid them altogether. Most professionals will only use one or two throughout the whole book. They use body language instead to show what the character is feeling or how they are delivering their dialogue. I use them occasionally if the situation calls for it, but try to keep them at a minimum.

Don't Stop to Correct Mistakes

Until You Finish Your FIRST Draft.

Keep typing while the creative juices are flowing. Often it pays to let it sit for a few days after, even a week, or more, then go back over it again. You'll be more likely to catch mistakes you didn't notice before.

Too often our brain will "auto-correct" and we tend to read what is *supposed* to be there, rather than what *actually is* there. Because of our brain's tendency to "auto-correct" we often miss small errors.

Give a couple of copies of your manuscript to friends who are knowledgeable about writing. The idea is, you want someone who will be truthful, but not vicious. This is why it is good to join a writer's group and have critique sessions. The more eyes you have to read your material, the better to catch errors.

Not only to catch typos and other errors, but to tell you if your plot points need beefing up, if some sections are too wordy and need to be tightened. Or if you need more detail for clarification. Or, if you need to pick up the pace in certain sections.

Avoid close friends or family, as they will most likely tell you that your writing is wonderful. They don't want to hurt your feelings. A writers group will give you good advice on what you might need to make your story more publishable. Even my multi-published friends (some with 5 to 12 books published) depend on our critique group to help spot problems.

A book is never written in just one draft. Your first draft is your rough draft. You should plan on doing *several drafts,* at the very least, and possibly dozens, before your work is honed and polished enough to present to an agent or acquiring editor.

It is through the revision, re-writing, and editing process where the REAL writing takes place. That's when you look for that perfect verb rather than the generic one, you watch for those repetitive, favorite words that pop up several times on a page. And the many other things, that would take another book to tell about all of them.

When I talk about an "editor," I usually mean an *acquiring editor* at a publishing house. The decision maker. If you need help in editing your manuscript **before** sending it off, there are many "independent editors" whom you can pay to do an edit. They either charge by the hour, or by the page, or by the project.

You can save a lot of money by learning the basics of grammar and punctuation yourself. Or many writers will exchange with each other and trade work. But you have to be willing to reciprocate. Or you'll find no one will be willing to help you, if you aren't willing to help them.

Editing can be very tedious and time consuming. That's why professional editors charge so much. It's not just the story in general that they are looking at, but they have to look at every comma, and punctuation, every word to make sure it fits the sentence, the right verb tense, that the grammar is correct, etc.

It is a good idea to get a good ***critique*** somewhere along the way, usually after the first couple of drafts, to make sure there are no plot holes. That certain scenes or chapters are working to advance the plot, to check for pacing, or other problems.

If you need to know if your plot is working, or if your characters are acting like they should under the circumstances of the story, or if the pacing is good, etc., then you might consider a "**Critique**," rather than an edit.

This is why it is good to find a critique group where you feel comfortable and have sections of your manuscript critiqued as you work on it. You can learn more about what is working and what is not working from a critique group than having a hundred editors looking for stray commas or grammar problems.

When you've done all this, then the edit is the final thing you do. Then you go back and make corrections based on the edits.

Use Your Spell Check.

After you've finished your first draft, go back and look for words you may have used wrong. If you type in a wrong word, but it is spelled correctly, your spell check won't catch it. I tend to invert letters when I type, and often "*so*" becomes typed in as "*do*." Or "*from*" becomes "*form*." Therefore, I have to go back and check to make sure it is the word I want.

Also, should it be *to, too, or two?* Did you mean *break,* or *brake?* Did you want *lightning, or lightening? There, their, or they're? Further or Farther?*

Many of these words sound alike and look alike, but have **different meanings**. If you aren't sure, then look them up.

Not using the right word can let the agent or editor know that you haven't learned the basics of grammar and writing. These things were taught in grade school. So, if you aren't sure, maybe take a refresher course, or at least have a good reference book handy.

You always have to **be willing to go back and** *re-read what you've written*.

An agent or editor won't work with a writer who is not willing to make changes or revisions to make their story stronger and more saleable.

Don't be so in love with every word you write that you can't delete something or change something if it is not working.

There is a **big difference** between "Artistic Value" or "Artistic Content," and plain **BAD** writing.

Remember, it is **not** the Editor's job at a publishing house to correct your mistakes. In this case "Editor" is a **title of position**, as in Acquisitions. Similar to the Editor of a Newspaper. They decide which articles or stories to print in the newspaper. The Acquiring Editor at a publishing house decides what books they want to take on and if they will make money for the publishing company. They still have to get it passed by the board. But they will go to bat for you if they like your work.

Competition is fierce for the few slots open on publisher's lists; therefore, they are more likely to take on a writer who knows the basics of good writing.

Also, it is **not up to the agent to fix all your mistakes either**. Too often a new writer believes that "with the help of the agent, they can get their manuscript up to publishable standards."

They expect the agent to go through draft after draft, *without pay*, acting as an editor, to improve their manuscript. This is basically expecting the agent to **co-author** their project, but then only collect their agent fee **IF** it sells. Or to edit their book for free.

This is not much of an incentive for an agent to take on a project that may require a lot of work. They get dozens of skillfully written manuscripts from writers who know the basics.

Agents don't have the time to "teach" new writers HOW to write. Especially, when it can take *years* to learn and hone the craft.

You may have the most wonderful story, but if it is riddled with errors, mistakes, and the writing quality is poor, they *will not read enough of it* to find out if it is good or not. It will go into the rejection pile.

As I mentioned before, editing can be very tedious and time consuming. So don't expect an agent to do all this work for free. If you want a quality edit, you have to pay a professional for their time.

A Word About Chapter Length.

Keep chapters somewhere between 6 pages at the shortest and no more than 20 pages at the longest. If they run too short, then maybe they should be scene breaks, instead. Somewhere around 10 to 15 pages is a good average. If they run too long, the reader gets tired. For some Historical novels they can run a bit longer. But it's a good idea to keep them within a manageable range. Some writers, like Mary Higgins Clark, are noted for their short chapters of just one to three pages. And this is okay too. As long as it fits the pattern. But don't have real long chapters, then some real short chapters. Be consistent. However, they don't have to conform to a specific page count.

Remember, the reader's eye needs a break, too. If you have chapters going on for longer than 20 pages, then maybe find a place to break them up into separate chapters.

And **remember to end your chapter with a good hook** to pull the reader forward and to keep them reading.

Chapters and File Management.

It is best to have about four chapters per file. I used to have each chapter as a separate file, but this can get tedious when changing page numbers and printing out a whole manuscript, especially if you've done a lot of revisions. However, it is a good idea to **keep the first three chapters in a separate file** since this is what most editors or agents will ask for first. Usually the first three chapters and a full synopsis. Include with these the Prologue, Foreword, Preface, Author's Note, or any other writing that would come before your first chapter.

However, do **NOT** include a Table of Contents, or Dedication Page, or Acknowledgment Pages. These don't tell the editor or agent anything about your writing skills.

Usually before an editor or agent asks for the full manuscript, they want to see if you have honed your writing skills first. If they like what they read, and you have skillfully pulled them into your story, they will ask for the full manuscript.

The Table of Contents, Dedication Page, and Acknowledgements will go in when the *book is close to being printed*. You should not include these pages as part of your manuscript submission.

After the first three chapters (include with this anything that comes in front, such as a Prologue, that pertains to the story itself), put the rest in files of about **four**

chapters per file, or roughly about 40 to 50 pages per file. I wouldn't type your manuscript as **one long file**, because *if for some reason it should get deleted*, this could be disastrous. I've had this happen before. It is much easier to re-type a few chapters than a whole 400 page manuscript. Therefore, I suggest you break them up into groups of four or five chapters per file.

However, if you back them up on a flash drive or other means, then you should keep them all together as a full manuscript. Some use the "Cloud" or other on-line storage systems.

Keep your **title page in a separate file**, because you usually have to go back in and change the word count. Also, it messes up if you want to print out your first chapter and it will often print a page number and header on your title page.

Your title page does NOT count as page one of your story.

Page one starts where your story starts. Either the first page of Chapter One, or the first page of the Prologue. Also, the title page *does not count as part of your word count* for your manuscript. That's why it is often easier to have the title page in a different file than the rest of your manuscript.

Always <u>include</u> a Title Page with anything you send out. Even if you're only sending out the first three chapters. It just looks more professional. For more information, see the section below on **How to Format a Title Page**.

Keep your **synopsis** in a separate file, also. It is a good idea to *have a long synopsis* and *a short synopsis*. Short being from 1 to 4 pages single-spaced. Long

being from 4 to 10 pages double-spaced. I wouldn't go over 10 double-spaced pages.
If your synopsis is going over 10 pages, then you are trying to rewrite your book. Most
editors or agents prefer the shorter the better. Tell your story in a nut shell. This is the
one time you get to tell, rather than show.

Word Count.

If you are using the proper format with the correct margins, the right font and the correct point typeface, an average 300 page manuscript should equal roughly 75,000 words or a bit higher (in the **Courier font**). A 320 page manuscript equals approximately 80,000 words. A 350 page manuscript equals about 87,500 words. And a 400 page manuscript equals about 100,000 words. This is if you are going by the average of <u>250 words per manuscript page</u> in the **Courier font**.

When using the **Times New Roman** font, the average word count may be around 300 words per page. Take your page count, and times it by the average number of words per page (usually 250 to 300) and this will give you the **estimated word count** that editors often go by.

However, these days, you can click on **File** at the top of your screen (usually upper left corner) then scan down to **Properties** and click on that. If you go to the tab marked **Information**, it should bring up the word count for the document you are working on. Total these up for the full manuscript and you will have your computer word count.

Don't confuse **word count** with character count. The character count doesn't tell them anything.

These days, if you use *Microsoft Word*, you can see your word count on the bottom left side of the screen.

The word count on your computer will usually be somewhat different than the estimated count. The reason they go by the manuscript word count is that this allows for spaces between chapters, dialogue, etc. They have to fit your manuscript into a certain amount of space when publishing your book and this is their usual rule of thumb.

This is especially true for short stories where space is even more limited. If you are submitting a short story for publication, be sure to stay within the word count limits. They plan their space very carefully and if you go over their suggested amount, you may find a rejection slip in the mail. Or they may ask you to trim it down in order to meet their allotted space.

When giving your word count to the editor or agent, for novels, round your word count to the nearest 1,000 words. For novellas, or short stories of about 50 pages, round to the nearest 500 words, anything up to 50 pages, round to the nearest 100 words, and if it is less than 20 pages round to the nearest 50 or even 10 words. If a periodical has a specific word count, then your story needs to fit within that range, but **never go over** the specified word count. Learn to say a lot in a few words.

Many publishers will now use your computer word count. But, it's a good idea to know the old rule of thumb estimation as well.

Most **publishers have specific guidelines for word count** and won't accept anything that goes over that, or below it. An average novel should run between 80,000 words to 90,000 words. If you are too much over 100K, then you are getting too long and might need to tighten down your story. Also, if it is too short, it may not be acceptable either.

Be aware that many agents will not handle short stories, poetry, novellas, or article length material as they are not cost effective.

For instance, let's say you get paid $100 for your short story, which is actually a lot these days. The 15% or $15 the agent earns is hardly worth all the time, effort, and postage in sending out your short story time and time again.

The pay actually averages around $10 to $35 depending on the length. And many only pay you with "copies" of the publication rather than any money. So, you can see there is not much incentive for an agent to take on these shorter types of material.

However, even for these short types of material, any editors where you might send your work will still expect you to know the basics of proper formatting. Even a short 5 page manuscript should be formatted the same way as a novel manuscript.

Know Your Genre.

Know what the rules are for the genre you write in. Find out what the average word count is for books or stories within your genre. Most publishers have specific guidelines for their different imprints. For instance: Most suspense novels will start at about 80,000 words to about 90,000. Therefore, your manuscript must fit within those guidelines and not be much over, or under their specified word count. Some historical novels may run somewhat longer, around 100,000 to 130,000.

Maybe a beach-read or cozy mystery might be a bit shorter, at around 60,000 to 70,000 words. Also a contemporary romance might run about that same word count. If your story runs at only 50,000 words or shorter, then it may be too short for the publisher's guidelines.

However, Harlequin Romances can run about 45,000 to 65,000. They are pretty short and have to fit a formula. Depending on which line you send to. Thus the genre, "formula romance."

Do a bit of research before you send off your material to see if your word count fits your target publisher's guidelines. If your manuscript is more than 150,000 words, you are getting much too long. Anything over 100K is considered long. I sometimes get submissions at over 200,000 or 300,000 words. These could easily be broken down into two or three books.

Most publishers will not take on a manuscript of this size by an unknown writer. A well-known writer can get away with this, but seldom will a new, unpublished, or unknown author be able to interest a publisher in a work of this length.

For children's stories, you would **format your manuscript exactly the same way as a novel**. Do NOT use novelty fonts or colored paper. Keep it professional. Keep in mind that most publishers of children's books have their own "in-house illustrators," therefore, you don't need to worry about illustrations for your picture book.

However, if you want to team up with a talented artist, make sure the art work looks **professional**. Never submit original artwork. Only send copies that will fit within the pages of your manuscript. On 8 ½ by 11 inch standard paper. No large pages of artwork.

For non-fiction books, you still format your manuscript the same way as outlined above. If accepted for publication, it will be re-formatted according to the editor's and printer's specifications.

Watch for "Widows."

A "Widow" is when one or two words are left over from the previous page, and left dangling there all by themselves at the top of the next page. Most professional writers try to eliminate them.

Save these for when you believe you are nearing your **final draft** and are about ready to send it out. Go through your manuscript, page by page and look for these at the top of pages. Most of the new writing programs or software has what is called an "end wrap." This will automatically take care of this problem.

But if you chose not to use this feature, or you don't have this feature, there are several things you can do. This is so you don't have that single short line or one word left over on the last page of a chapter, left sitting there all by itself on an otherwise blank page. That's why it is called a "widow."

Look for paragraphs where you can rewrite to eliminate one or two words, thus moving the text up, or add a few words or a sentence or two, to extend the text down by one line. This will move the lines up or down on the page.

Maybe you can split a longer paragraph into two to move the lines down, or combine two short paragraphs to move a line upward.

These days many word processors will automatically <u>wrap lines</u> and adjust the bottom margin for this, but sometimes you'll end up with a two or three inch bottom margin on one page that looks out of place. So it is a good idea to go through your manuscript and look for these to see where you can adjust a line here and there to eliminate the "widows." Or at least adjust the 3 inch bottom margin that looks out of place. Your manuscript will look all the more professional because you've taken the time to do this.

<u>The</u> **exception** to this would be where there is a short sentence, such as a short snappy line of dialogue, which has one or two words, but is its **"own" paragraph**.

Then this is okay. (Like this.)

Or as in short dialogue:

"Thanks," John said.

The short line above is its **own** paragraph.

If the top type goes all or most of the way across the page, then it is usually okay to leave it. You will seldom see a *widow* in a published book. Even though you are only sending out a manuscript, you should still try to eliminate these, as it will make your manuscript look more polished and professional.

I often point these out to writers who have sent off their finished manuscript to me. I know that editors look for them when reading a submission. So be aware of the "Widows."

Save Everything on a Backup Disk.

I usually have one novel per disk and everything that pertains to that novel, such as a long and short synopsis, any query letters, research notes, plot and character notes, etc. Don't mix and match novels or stories on a disk unless they are related in some way. It can get confusing.

You can also use a thumb drive or external hard drive to save everything as well. But be aware that **these can <u>crash</u>, too**. A friend of mine found out the hard way that thumb drives **can** crash when she lost her 400 page manuscript. She was able to take the drive to a tech person and restore some of it, but had to retype most of it over again. And she had a publisher waiting for it.

Other ways to keep a safe copy is to **email a copy to yourself or a friend** so that you can access it from another computer if you have to.

Also, **keep a current print-out or paper copy of your manuscript**. This is in case your computer crashes, or a file or a disk gets erased. You might have to type it all back in later on. **And accidents do happen**. Stacking trays are wonderful for storing printed copies.

And whenever possible, print out your working drafts on the backs of older drafts. Recycle paper when you can. I never print out working drafts on good paper.

Save the good paper for when you're ready to start sending it out. This should be many drafts later. And use your draft mode when printing out chapters that you plan to edit or give to a reader for critiquing. This saves on ink as well. Wait until you feel your manuscript is honed, professional and polished, then print out on good paper and in the darker or standard text mode.

When you print out your final draft, print on <u>ONE SIDE</u> of the paper only. Make sure your manuscript looks neat, is properly formatted, and reads and looks professional.

Never send out anything that isn't your best work.

HINT: For new or unknown writers, it is best to <u>finish your novel and have it honed and polished and edited</u> before sending it out, or submitting to an editor or agent. Don't send out a rough draft. This makes a bad first impression.

Suppose an editor likes the first part and says, "Send me the whole manuscript."

If you have to hurry and finish your novel, it may not be your best work and will most likely lack polishing. Also, you want to make sure it is free of spelling errors, typos, punctuation errors, and other manuscript problems. Acquiring Editors don't have time to work with amateur writers to help them get their stories and manuscripts up to publishable standards

You will be expected to polish your writing skills yourself, especially if you want to break in with traditional publishing. If you aren't sure of your writing, then have it edited by a qualified service or professional editor.

Basically, agents and editors expect you to hone your craft yourself. *There is much more to writing than just putting words down on the page.*

For more information on writing, see my book: ***"A Hand Book For Writers, Plotting and Characters, Plus Many Writing Dos and Don'ts."*** There is more information at the end of this book.

Following these guidelines won't guarantee your work will get published. You still need a solid presentation and a good writing style. But it is much more impressive when an editor or literary agent sees a properly formatted manuscript when they first take it out of that envelope.

After all, they see the **physical look** of the manuscript **BEFORE** they even read one word of your story. Think first impressions. You want to get off to a good start with that agent or acquiring editor.

The Following Advice is Useful When

Approaching Editors and Agents:

<u>Always</u> enclose a <u>Self-Addressed, Stamped Envelope</u> (SASE)

for a reply. Otherwise you probably won't get one. Remember, ***the author <u>always</u> pays for the postage, BOTH ways.*** This is referred to as the **SASE**. So when an agent or editor says in their submission guidelines to include an **SASE**, in with your query or sample chapters, they are referring to the **Self-Addressed, Stamped Envelope**.

If you want your sample chapters or full manuscript returned, make sure you enclose an envelope ***large enough and with enough postage***. I've had writers send a <u>full manuscript</u> in a large Mylar envelope, and enclose a small 9 by 12 inch envelope, with the postage attached, for the return of their **full** manuscript. There is no way that a 350 page manuscript would fit into an envelope of that size.

They never took the time to test it, *to make sure it would fit* in the return envelope. What were they thinking? Some people are unclear on the concept.

And once the postage is stuck on the envelope, I can't transfer it to another one. The post office won't accept it that way. If I were only returning the first few chapters, that size of envelope would work fine, but not for a *full* manuscript.

If you don't need your sample chapters returned, **then enclose a self-addressed #10 business size envelope with a stamp on it for a reply.**

Hint: Do <u>not</u> use metered postage on your return envelope, as this goes stale the same day as issued with the date on it. Use stamps only.

Most agents or editors will have a backlog of material and replies can run anywhere from a couple of weeks to several months, depending on their backlog. Agents do not spend hours on the phone calling people to tell them they've been rejected, or even if they are interested in seeing more of your story. Nor do we spend hours on line emailing rejections.

Most likely in the event of a rejection you may get a form letter. If you do get a few personal comments, either in the letter or on the manuscript pages, take them to heart. Remember, they know what sells, what works and what doesn't.

Most agents would go broke if they were expected to provide postage for hundreds of rejections each month. Therefore, it is the <u>industry standard</u> that if you want a reply, you should provide a return envelope with your name and address on the front. With a **stamp** in the top right corner.

Occasionally I would get a return envelope with **my name** and address on the front. The reason you put **your own** address on the front is so you get a reply sent back to **you**.

Most agents don't like cold calls.

This interrupts their work and makes them cranky. And as far as editors are concerned, unless you know their extension number, you won't get through. Or unless they recognize your name, you won't get through. They consider cold calls from writers who want to pitch their book about as welcome as a pesky telemarketer.

Your best foot in the door is a well-written, polished, and properly formatted manuscript with a great story or plot and interesting characters. If you need to know some information, then email them with a question. This way they can get back to you when it's convenient for them.

For more information on this topic, see my book: ***"How to Write an Effective Query Letter," Plus Other Advice on Approaching Agents and Editors***. (More information is at the end of this book)

Next I will cover how to format a title page.

Many writers don't know how to properly format a title page, or what to put on a title page, other than the title.

The title page should contain some **specific information**.

How to Format a Title Page

It is best to keep your title page in a separate file than the rest of your book. **The title page *does NOT count as Page 1 of your story, nor as part of your word count.* It should not contain a header or page number.**

In the upper left-hand corner of your title page, type in:

Your name,

Address,

Phone number, and

Email address.

Sometimes you can include an alternate phone number, such as a cell phone.

This can be single-spaced, and in the same font as the rest of your manuscript. If your manuscript is printed in Courier font, then your title page should be too. If you use Times New Roman, then use this font on your title page.

Be sure to *use your real name* in the upper left corner, **not** a pen name here. Basically this is where all your contact information goes in case they like your work and want to get ahold of you. If accepted by the publisher, this is the name they make your advance check out to. Or royalty checks to as well.

Do NOT put your social security number with your personal information. If they need it for any reason, they will ask for it. Wait until they are offering you a contract or a check first. These days with identity theft running rampant, it is not a good idea to put your social security number out there for just anyone to copy.

Do NOT use the copyright symbol © or type the word Copyright on the title page.

This is the sign of an amateur. Amateurs will often load up their title page and sometimes the manuscript pages with copyright symbols, First North American Rights, numbers or dates. **<u>You don't need this</u>**.

Basically, anything that comes out of your computer is automatically copyrighted. Once something is fixed in tangible form, it is copyrighted. This was made into law in the mid 1980's after computers became more common. Computers automatically date your files and various drafts, so that because of this, you can prove in most any court when you started working on a particular draft of your story.

Once accepted for publication, usually **the publisher will *formally* copyright** your work **for you** as part of the process and put it into one of the first pages of your book. If you want to go ahead and copyright your material yourself, then do so, but don't load up your manuscript with all the dates, etc. You don't need it and it just marks your manuscript as amateurish.

Authors **own** the property, their creations. The publisher is **licensing** the right to profit from your property. Authors are advised to never sell or give up their Copyright.

Also, you may wind up doing several revisions and re-writes to suit an editor, and it is usually only the *final version* of your story you want to have formally Copyrighted. This is the version that will appear on store shelves. Even though you go through a publisher, you still own the Copyright for your work.

When a publisher formally Copyrights your work, it still belongs to <u>you</u>. They are just protecting their investment in you as the author. And the Copyright is formally filed in your behalf. They do this for all their authors. Therefore, it is the amateur writer who loads up their manuscript with all kinds of symbols and dates.

Keep in mind that **Titles, or ideas, cannot be Copyrighted**.

The Copyright protects the ***words <u>inside</u>*** the book itself from being plagiarized. But **you can't Copyright the idea for the book, nor the title**. That's why you will often see the same title for other books. And many writers will come up with similar storylines, but done a bit differently. As they say, there are no new stories. Just rehashed ones with a new twist.

Copyright information should NOT appear on your manuscript pages, or in the header or the footer, either.

Hint: Never sell your Copyright to the publisher; otherwise you do give up all your rights to that work.

Normally the publisher pays you for the ***rights to publish your work***. They don't own the copyright, <u>you</u> do. They are licensing the right to make money from your work.

However, some publishers will only pay a flat fee for a particular work, in which case you don't get any royalties after that. Often when this happens, they will buy the Copyright outright.

This is different from when submitting an article to a periodical or newspaper. Usually you have the right to re-use your information in your article and can revamp and submit it to any number of other publications.

By the way, **the length of a copyright is the lifetime of the author plus 70 years.** (It used to be 50 years, but was recently increased and made into law by the family of Margaret Mitchell the author of "Gone With the Wind") After that it becomes public domain. That's why anyone can re-print a copy of the older classics (such as Shakespeare, Homer, etc.) for distribution and sale. But don't try to pass these off as your own work.

NEXT: Center the <u>title</u> on the page.

This can be done in **bold** and in CAPS. You don't have to have it in 70 point type face. Just normal 12 point is fine. If you want it a bit larger, then go to about 15 or 20 points. Just don't go overboard. Again, don't use fancy fonts or colored paper. Stick to a professional looking title page.

No pictures or cover art work. They have departments to design their covers. If accepted, they might ask for your opinion, but they make the final decision as to the cover design.

In fact, you may not keep your title. It they don't like your title, they will come up with a new one. Publishers have marketing departments that do this as well.

Beneath the title, **center the word "by" with a <u>lower case "b."</u>** This should be a double-spaced line below the title.

Then **<u>center your name under this</u>**. These should all be double-spaced lines. **<u>If you are using a pen name</u>** for any reason, this is where you would type it. Your name can be in bold. Or you can **use your *pen name* below your real name**, as in: Writing as John Smith, or AKA John Smith, or Pen Name: John Smith.

Next, **go down two double-spaced lines**, and center the cursor and **type in the genre**.

The genre is the type of story you write. Romance, Science Fiction, Fantasy, Western, Historical, Thriller, Mystery, Suspense, Main Stream Fiction, or Non-Fiction, etc. Include any sub-genre, such as Romantic Thriller, Historical Romance, Romantic Suspense, etc. if applicable to your genre.

If you're not sure where yours fits in, maybe take a look at book store shelves and see where they have similar books listed on the shelves.

This information is important to the editor or agent as it tells them if your story fits the type of material they handle. For instance, don't send out a Sci-fi or fantasy if an agent doesn't handle that type of material. The same with a publisher. Do some research and make sure they take on your type of material before you send it to them.

On the next line, below your genre, center and **type in the approximate word count**.

Don't put the exact word count (81,213). Round it to the nearest 1,000 words for novels (81,000+); the nearest 500 for longer short stories, or novellas; the nearest 100 for short stories of about 20 pages, and so on.

For shorter stories or articles round to the nearest 50; and anything under 10 pages, round to the nearest 10 words or even 5 words. In other words, the shorter the word count, the nearer it should be rounded. *Never go over* the publisher's suggested guidelines.

You might include the finished **page count** below the word count, but editors and agents **go by <u>word count</u>**. Do **not** include the amount of **characters**. This doesn't tell them anything.

Therefore, all your information should be on the Title Page that an agent or editor needs: your contact information, the title, the genre, and the word count.

If you are reading this as an **eBook**, it may not look like it should for a normal 8 ½ x 11 inch printed page. But with the explanations, you should get the idea of how a proper title page should be set up.

If you are reading this in a **print version**, then see the next page for how your information should look in the upper LEFT corner of the title page:

Tina Foster

1234 Elm Street

Anytown, Utah 84123

Phone: (801) 555-2013

Cell: (801) 555-1234

Email: Writer@aol.com

THIS IS MY BOOK

by

Tina Foster

Romantic Thriller

Approximately 81,000+ Words

If you have a literary agent
you would put their contact
information in the right side lower
corner. Include their
email address and web page.

The following is how the manuscript pages should look:

CHAPTER ONE

Example of a Manuscript Page

If you are reading this in a printed version, it should be self-explanatory. However, nothing on this page will look like it should when published in eBook format. But imagine it as set for double-spaced type and with no justification so that the right side margin is ragged, not flush.

Also, the first line of each new paragraph is indented. Remember to space down 5 double-spaced lines to start your chapter heading. You can space down 8 blank lines as well, or even 10 is okay, too.

The **Header** should contain the title in caps in the left-hand corner followed by a slash (/) and your last name. The reason for this is so the agent or editor can find which package your manuscript goes back to when they finish reading it.

With no title or last name, they won't know who wrote it and what return envelope it goes back in to. Also, editors and agents like the page numbers at the *top* of the page, *not* at the bottom of the page, so that everything is there at a glance. They won't have to search all over the page for basic information.

You wouldn't believe how many manuscripts I get that have no header or page numbers on it at all. Accidents happen. If the pages get dropped or shuffled, I would not be able to put them back in the correct order. Therefore, it is very important to include consecutive page numbers on each Manuscript Page. Again, do not put a header or page numbers on your title page.

For printing on 8 ½ x 11 inch paper, be sure to set your margins at 1.25 inches instead of just one inch. Wide margins are very much appreciated by editors. It allows more room for writing comments in the margins, and making editing notes.

Look for the other books in my series, on writing, with subjects such as: **<u>A Hand Book For Writers</u>** which includes Plotting and Characters, and the many Dos and Don'ts of Writing, and many other things that editors look for in great writing.

I taught Fiction Writing classes for ten years and these books contain most of the subjects I taught in those classes. I decided to put it into these books to make it easier for writers to learn.

Also, **<u>How to Write an Effective Query Letter</u>**, includes more advice on approaching editors and agents. As well as how to write a working synopsis.

A valuable book is, **<u>Ten Reasons Why Editors and Agents Stop Reading</u>**.

Notice I've used <u>underlining</u> in this manuscript sample instead of my Italics setting for these few paragraphs.

If you think you are going to save time and money by emailing sample chapters, think again. Many legitimate agents don't like emails with sample chapters or emailed attachments.

For one thing, **they don't like email "attachments"** due to the risk of new types of virus, worms, trojans or other computer problems. Many an agent's computer has crashed because of a downloaded virus from sample chapters. They don't know you, and don't have any reason to trust that you didn't include a worm, trojan, or virus with your attachment. No matter how up to date an agent's virus protections is, there are always new and dangerous ones being developed all the time.

Another reason sample chapters by email are not popular with agents, is because they don't like to sit at their computer and read for hours at a time. For myself, I prefer a comfy chair with good lighting, and take a stack of manuscripts to read through. Also, most agents and editors receive hundreds of queries each month. It may take them several weeks to several months to get to yours.

By including sample chapters with your emailed query it might just guarantee a quicker rejection, as they don't want to bother reading through it during their brief time on the computer. They usually have stacks of submissions where writers have taken the time and effort to mail them as per industry protocol.

Another problem with sample chapters sent by email is that the agent can't tell if your manuscript is properly formatted, how wide your margins are, if you have a proper header, etc. When someone emails writing samples, I'll often get chapters where each new paragraph is not indented on the first line. Therefore, you can't tell where one paragraph ends and another starts. It all looks like one long continuous block of text, which is very uninviting to the reader. Remember, editors and agents enjoy a pleasing looking manuscript. Some manuscripts don't translate well when sent by email.

Most editors at the larger publishers <u>will not accept email queries,</u> nor sample chapters by email <u>at all</u>. Most submissions <u>must be printed out</u> in proper format and sent <u>through the mail with an enclosed SASE return envelope.</u>

It is in <u>extremely bad taste</u> to expect an agent to print out **<u>your</u>** manuscript using **<u>their</u>** <u>own ink and paper</u>. It should go without saying that you <u>never fax</u> a manuscript to an agent, for the same reason.

However, to retract some of what I've said above, these days, many editors and agents have "gone green" in that they **will** accept emailed submissions of chapters, but normally you will have to paste the sample chapters into the body of the emailed query, rather than be sent as an attachment.

You will have to ask each agent you query if this is okay. Most agents or editors have a **web page** with their **submission guidelines** listed, telling how they like your submissions presented.

Take time to learn industry protocol and you'll have a much better chance of looking like a professional.

Of course, you need to hone your writing skills as well, but by taking the time to learn proper formatting you will be that much farther ahead than those who don't.

*   *   *

I hope these suggestions will help to make your manuscript look and read more polished and professional.

Best of luck to you with your project.

Tina Foster

Foster Literary Agency

Email: fosterliterary@yahoo.com

I am now in the process of phasing down my literary agency in preparation for retirement. I would like to spend more time on my own writing, and maybe do some independent editing and critiquing for other writers who need a little help.

I am currently offering a **Critiquing Service** for those who wish to take advantage of my years of experience. You can have just the first 5 or 10 pages, or 20 pages critiqued, or the first chapter or first three chapters.

I can usually tell within those first few pages or chapters what problems you might be having with your presentation and writing style. Most all problems tend to be consistent throughout the entire manuscript. For more information, and details on how to send your material for this service, feel free to email me, or visit my web site at: www.tinafosterauthor.com.

For more information on my critiquing service, email me at: http:/fosterliterary@yahoo.com.

Take advantage of the other books in my series on writing:

"Ten Reasons Why Editors, and Agents Stop Reading."

Learn the ten most common mistakes writers make which can cause an acquiring editor at a publishing house, or literary agent, to stop reading your manuscript an pick up someone else's.

"A Handbook For Writers," Plotting and Characters, Plus Many Writing Dos and Don'ts.

There is much more to writing than just putting words down on the pages. Amateur writers often have pages filled with common mistakes that tell the editor at a publishing house, or a literary agent, that they have not honed their writing skills, and their manuscript usually lacks polishing. The truth is, you get from 1 to 5 pages to hook that editor or agent into your story. If they aren't pulled in within those few pages, they will toss your manuscript and go on to the next one in their slush pile. Learn what things to avoid in your writing that turn off editors and agents. Learn the many dos and don'ts that editors and agents look for in great writing.

"How to Write an Effective Query Letter," Plus Other Advice on Approaching Editors and Agents.

There are dos and don'ts that editors and agents look for when vying for their interest in your project. Learn the best ways to approach them, and what turns them off.

All of these books are available as **eBooks** for Kindle. Save money by downloading on your Kindle or other eReader.

Visit my **author page** on Amazon to take a look inside any of my books. Just click on the cover to sample it, or to download or purchase.

http://www.amazon.com/author/fostertina.

I now have a romantic suspense out, *Flirting With Danger*.

Witness to a murder . . . Stalked by the killers . . . Who will save her?

Lovers of suspense, thrillers, romance, action, and crime fiction will enjoy this fast-paced and tension-filled novel.

Warning: Contains some R-rated adult scenes.

I hope you find the information in this book helpful in getting your manuscript to look inviting and professional.

Good Luck and Good Writing!